A STRAIGHTFORWARD GUIDE TO

SMALL CLAIMS IN THE COUNTY COURT

PETER WHIMSTER

STRAIGHTFORWARD PUBLISHING LIMITED

A Straightforward Guide to Small Claims in the County Court
First published in the United Kingdom by

Straightforward Publishing Limited
38 Cromwell Road
London E17 9NJ

© Peter Whimster 1995
First Edition

All rights reserved. No part of this publication may be reproduced, stored in a database or retrieval system or reproduced in any form or in any way, electronically, mechanically, print, fotoprint, microfilm, or any other means without the prior written permission of the publisher.

British Library Cataloguing in Publication data. A catalogue record of this book is available from the British Library.

ISBN 0-9521133 7 9

Typeset and layout by Tim Parkin, London
Cover design by Neil Grant, Front Line Graphics, Brighton
Printed by BPC Wheaton, Exeter

Contents

INTRODUCTION TO THIS GUIDE 1
    Forms 2
    Rules of the County Court 2
    Gender 3

1.
TYPES OF SMALL CLAIM 5
    The Suppliers Right to Payment 5
    The Purchaser's Rights 5
    Sale Of Goods Act – 1979 6
    Supply of Goods and Services Act – 1982 6
    Cheques Act – 1957 & 1982 7
    Unfair Contract Terms Act – 1977 7
    Personal Injuries 7
    Consumer Protection Act – 1987 8
    The Occupier's Liability Act – 1957 8
    Key Points 9

2.
THE SMALL CLAIMS COURT
& ARBITRATION 11
    Prevent Claims Arising – Pre-Emptive Action 11
    When You Experience a Problem 12
    Steps You Should Take Before Taking Legal Action 12
    Considerations Before Taking Someone To Court 12
    Key Points 14

3.
TYPES OF COUNTY COURT ACTION 15
    Explanation of a Default Summons 15

Types of County Court Summons...............................15
Key Points...14

4.
AN OVERVIEW OF PROCEDURE..............................17
Issue a Default Summons...17
Court Service..18
Forms of Admission..18
Defence and Counterclaim (Forms N9A and N9B) 18
Admission or Partial Admission......................................18
Defence..19
Counterclaim 19
Date of the Arbitration Hearing....................................19
Directions Issued by the Court 20
Disclosure of Evidence..20
Enforcement Proceedings..20
Key Points...21

5.
THE PLAINTIFF..23
Plaintiff's Name & Address...23
Defendant's Address..23
Category of Claim..23
Particulars of Claim..23
Particulars..24
What to do Next..25
Obtaining Judgement in Default.................................25
Accepting an Admission and Offer of Payment............26
Key Points...27

6.
THE DEFENDANT..37
Forms of Admission, Defence & Counterclaim............37

Form of Admission 38
Form of Defence 38
Preparing the Defence 39
Form of Counterclaim 39
Setting Aside a Default Judgement 40
Key Points 41

7.
ISSUES OF EVIDENCE 47
Types of Evidence 47
How to Use Your Evidence 48
Burden of Proof 48
Onus of Proof 48
What You Must Prove 49
Proof of Loss 50
Types of Evidence 50
Documentary Evidence 51
Witness Evidence 51
Expert Evidence 51
Costs of Witness and Experts 52
Key Points 53

8.
PREPARING FOR THE
ARBITRATION HEARING 55
Pre-Trial Reviews and Directions 55
Failure to Attend a Pre-Arbitration Appointment 56
Exchange of Evidence 56
Trial Date 56
Consent Orders 56
Withdrawing the Summons 57
Key Points 58

III

9.
ARBITRATION & JUDGEMENT 59
How to Present Your Case – The Plaintiff 60
How to Present Your Case – The Defendant 60
Failure to Attend 61
Judgement 61
Setting Aside a Default Judgement 61
Key Points 62

10.
ENFORCEMENT PROCEDURES 63
Enforcement Proceedings – Money Judgements 63
Oral Examination (Form N37/38) 63
Attachment of Earnings (Form N337) 63
Warrant of Execution (Form N323) 64
Garnishee Order (Forms N349) 64
Charging Order (N86/87) 64
Order for Sale 65
Appointment of a Receiver 65
Bankruptcy Proceedings 65
Choice of Method of Enforcement 65
Procedure for Obtaining Enforcement Orders 66
Key Points 67

GLOSSARY OF IMPORTANT TERMS 71

APPENDIX 1 77
Court Fees 77

APPENDIX 2 79
Order 19 (Reference to Arbitration) 79

APPENDIX 3 89
Forms reproduced in this guide 89

INTRODUCTION TO THIS GUIDE

This guide will outline the small claims procedure used in the County Court, known as "arbitration". Except for a brief summary in chapter 1, it will not outline "the law" or "your rights". The law is outside the scope of this guide, the aim of which is to detail how to enforce a "small claim". The small claims procedure is intended to be understood by the general public. The Court takes certain procedural steps on your behalf and the Court personnel advise on steps you must take.

In order to provide for cost effective resolutions of disputes, the local courts, known as County Courts, offer a simplified court procedure for resolving minor disputes. The procedure is known as "arbitration" and the minor disputes are called "small claims". A small claim is one which involves a sum of money below £1,000. It is expected that this level will be increased by the Lord Chancellor. The "small claims procedure" is designed to be "user friendly" so that a novice can make use of it and pursue a claim without legal representation. Examples of the forms used throughout an action are appended to the relevant chapters.

With the exception of the small claims procedure, our Legal System is "adversarial". This means that in a dispute, the aggrieved party, called the "plaintiff", must present a case against the offending party, known as the "defendant", to a Judge. The Judge will hear arguments from both sides and reach a decision. The decision of the Judge will take the form of a "judgement", which is a Court Order that requires certain action. The Defendant may be ordered to pay compensation known as "damages" to the Plaintiff. The Plaintiff is entitled to enforce the Judgement if the Defendant does not comply. This requires issuing "enforcement proceedings" against the Defendant.

A small claim is not heard in Open Court and the adversarial nature of the proceedings are replaced by a judge who will ask questions and help find a solution to the dispute. However, the Plaintiff must still present a case for the judge to accept or reject.

Under the small claims procedure, if you make a claim and lose, the person you are claiming against cannot recover their legal costs from you. The intention is that a small claim should be defended without legal representation.

We very much hope that this guide will prove to be invaluable to those who wish to pursue a claim or defend a claim, in the county courts.

If you have any comments concerning the contents and information in this book please do not hesitate to contact Straightforward Publishing at: 38 Cromwell Road, Walthamstow, London E17 9JN.

Forms

This guide contains county court forms printed by permission of the lord chancellor's department. Although care has been taken to reproduce the correct forms, the forms printed are reproduced to illustrate and explain the text. Care should be taken to collect the right forms from the court office and to use the correct forms in pursuing your claim or defending a claim against you. *All such forms are Crown Copyright and they are reproduced with the kind permission of the Controller of HMSO.*

Rules of the County Court

The procedure in this guide is derived from the Rules of the County Court Relating to Arbitration. The principal rule is Rule 19 which is printed in Appendix 2.

Gender

For convience, the masculine gender has been used throughout this book and is in no way intended to indicate bias or sexism.

Important Note: This guide applies to England & Wales. The law and procedure in Scotland & Northern Ireland is different and this guide should not be used in those countries.

1.
TYPES OF SMALL CLAIM

A Small Claim will most likely result from a breach of contract. This includes non-payment of an invoice which has been properly issued. A claim for payment is a simple matter involving a claim for financial compensation.

The Suppliers Right to Payment

Where goods are delivered or services rendered, the supplier or service provider is entitled to the agreed price or agreed payment for the service rendered. If no price has been agreed, the supplier or service provider is entitled to a reasonable sum for the goods supplied or service rendered.

The Purchaser's Rights

When goods are supplied which do not comply with the contract, or in breach of terms implied by the Sale of goods Act (see below), the purchaser is entitled to either:

- compensation known as "damages", or
- if the breach is serious, to reject the goods and claim damages for financial loss, for example, a refund of the purchase price, the cost above the agreed purchase price for replacement goods which comply with the terms of the contract, and any additional loss suffered. The compensation claimed would be the purchase price and any other additional loss suffered. In this situation, the contract is discharged, which means that the purchaser is released of his obligation of payment, or

- to reject the goods and affirm the contract, which means that the contract is not discharged and the purchaser requires the supplier to perform the contract and holds the supplier to his contractual obligations. If the contract is not performed, the aggrieved party may sue for breach of contract.

Sale Of Goods Act – 1979

The Sale of Goods Act implies certain terms into contracts for the sale of goods. This means that the seller must supply goods which satisfy certain statutory terms of contract imposed by Parliament. The principal implied terms are:

- the vendor must own the goods

- the goods must be of merchantable quality

- the goods must be fit for the purpose for which those goods are commonly supplied or for any specified purpose

If these conditions are not satisfied, the purchaser has the rights specified above, to damages, to rejection and damages, or to affirm the contract and claim damages for loss suffered.

Supply of Goods and Services Act – 1982

The supplier of services is entitled to payment of his invoice. However, the purchaser is entitled to work of a reasonable standard and a workman or service provider must use "reasonable skill and care" in undertaking work and complete the work within a "reasonable time". If work is not of a reasonable standard, and the purchaser must prove that this is the case, the supplier may be entitled to a reasonable payment.

The purchaser may be entitled to damages if the work is so substandard that financial loss is suffered, for example, in the case of re-plumbing or re-wiring which needs to be completely redone.

Cheques Act – 1957 & 1982

If a cheque is cancelled or dishonoured, the recipient can claim for breach of the Cheques Act. Very few defences exist and would include a fraudulent signature or that a cheque was signed under duress. If goods supplied were defective or not of merchantable quality, the defendant cannot resist a claim under the Cheques Act but must file a counter-claim instead of a defence.

Unfair Contract Terms Act – 1977

Contracts often include exclusion clauses, where one side attempts to limit its liability or the rights of the other party in the event of a breach of contract. The Unfair Contract Terms Act makes any clause excluding or limiting liability for death or personal injury void. Any exclusion clause which restricts or limits the terms implied by the Sale of Goods Act, where one party is dealing as a consumer, is void. This means that the exclusion has no effect. Any exclusion clause where one party is dealing on standard terms or one party is a business, will only be effective in so far as the person relying on it can prove that it is "reasonable" as defined by the Act.

Personal Injuries

The Lord Chancellor has encouraged and the Court of Appeal in a case called *Afzal - versus - Ford Motor Company Limited* has made it possible for minor personal injuries to be dealt with as a small claim, where the compensation claimed is less than £1,000. To succeed in a claim for personal injury, the plaintiff must prove that the defendant was negligent. Four issues must be proved by the plaintiff to establish negligence:

- that the defendant owed a duty of care
- the defendant acted in breach of his duty
- the breach caused the plaintiff's injury, and
- the injury was reasonably foreseeable, and not a "freak accident"

In the case of injury at work, the plaintiff could claim compensation if the defendant acted in breach of a statutory duty, of which there are many imposed by the Health & Safety At Work legislation.

These areas are complicated and research should be undertaken before taking legal action. However, a simple case could well be suited to the small claims procedure.

Consumer Protection Act – 1987

This act allows action against a "producer" of goods which are unsafe and cause personal injury or damage to property up to a maximum of £275.

The Occupier's Liability Act – 1957

This Act allows compensation for injury caused on land owned by another person or caused by unsafe buildings on such land. Trespassers do not have the same claim to compensation as lawful entrants on the land. The "occupier" is generally the owner of the land.

Now please read the **KEY POINTS** from chapter 1 overleaf.

KEY POINTS

- most small claims are for breach of contract

- small claims for personal injury caused by negligence or breach of statutory duty can be undertaken but the law is complicated and advice should be taken

2.
THE SMALL CLAIMS COURT & ARBITRATION

When a county court summons for £1,000 or less is issued, the dispute is categorised as a "small claim" and is automatically referred by the Court to "Arbitration". This in an informal procedure where a Judge hears each side of a dispute in a private room, rather than in an Open Court. Solicitors fees are not awarded to the successful party to an automatic Arbitration - unlike a hearing in Open Court. This is to encourage members of the public to conduct their own case.

The Court provides standard forms for completion by the opponents throughout a case with the intention that for simple matters, you could present your own case.

Prevent Caims Arising - Pre-Emptive Action

If you run a business, consider the benefits of a credit reference agency to check the creditworthiness of new customers. Reports can be obtained on-line via a computer and modem, for example, from Prestel. Depending on the service you are buying, ensure that you have a written contract or that you use your standard terms of business in a sale or purchase.

If you run a business and encounter serious problems in paying your creditors, always negotiate terms of payment and discuss your situation openly and honestly. Such action at an early stage often avoids legal proceedings being taken against you. Always keep your bank manager informed and up to date with your business affairs and avoid giving him unexpected surprises.

When You Experience a Problem

If you realise that a dispute is inevitable, ensure that you keep all relevant documents, such as a receipt for a payment, the contract, delivery note or any letters written. If you speak to anyone on the telephone, make a record of the person's name and of what was said. A case often turns on the documentary evidence available at the arbitration hearing and relevant documents with which you may have use to prove a case to the satisfaction of a judge usually come into existence before or during a dispute.

Steps You Should Take Before Taking Legal Action

The small claims court should be viewed as a last resort. Before issuing a Summons, an attempt should be made to reach a compromise by contacting the defendant. If no compromise or settlement is achieved, before issuing a Summons, you should write to the defendant threatening legal action and stating the financial recompense you are demanding. This is known as a "letter before action".

During the early stages when a compromise may be achieved, if you wish to make an offer which is not binding, your letter should be headed "without prejudice". If you intend to be held to an offer, for example, that you would accept a certain sum of money as compensation, you should not head the letter "without prejudice". Your letter would then be an open letter.

Considerations Before Taking Someone To Court

Before issuing a summons to enforce a debt or payment of an invoice, etc., consider whether the defendant is worth suing. If he is completely penniless, you may live a longer and more contented life if you decided not to take legal action. A credit reference agency will be able to give you some idea of the creditworthiness of a potential defendant.

Now please read the **KEY POINTS** from chapter 2 overleaf.

KEY POINTS

- take pre-emptive action in order to avoid recourse to law

- before issuing legal proceedings, make a complaint first

- if a dispute is inevitable, and cannot be solved by negotiation, keep copies of all relevant letters and documents

- even if you have a strong case, make sure that the defendant is worth suing. In some cases, it may be easier to walk away

- before issuing a summons, ensure that you know the legal ground for your claim. If you are unsure, obtain advice from a Citizens Advice Bureau, Law Centre, Trade Union, or contact the Consumers' Association, whose lawyers will give legal advice for a small monthly fee

- always write a letter before action before issuing a summons

- the County Court provides standard forms for issuing proceedings and the court staff will advise on procedure but cannot offer legal advice

3.
TYPES OF COUNTY COURT ACTION

The Small claims procedure applies to a type of claim known as a "default action". A Default Action is started by a Default Summons. Such a summons may be for either a specified sum of money under £1,000, or you could claim a sum which is under £1,000, but not know an exact figure. In those cases, where compensation is assessed, the level of compensation is determined by the judge who hears the case.

Explanation of a Default Summons

The significance of the term "default" is that, if the Defendant does not file a defence, the court will order judgement in your favour without a hearing. In other words, by issuing a default summons, the Defendant is summonsed to answer your claim and if he fails to do so by not filing a defence, the court will order judgement for the Plaintiff. In the case of a claim for a fixed amount, the court will order payment of that amount. If the amount is not specified, the court will order judgement for the plaintiff with damages to be assessed. A hearing date will be set for the assessment of damages.

Types of County Court Summons

There are two types of Default Summons form used by the County Court, one for a fixed claim (form N1) and the other for a damages to be assessed (form N2). These two forms are printed at the end of chapter five. Each form may be obtained at the Court Office.

Now please read the **KEY POINTS** from chapter 3 overleaf.

KEY POINTS

- first decide which type of action you are considering, either a fixed amount or damages to be assessed

- collect the right form from the court office

- you will be equipped to pursue an arbitration with the aid of this Guide. Other claims should be avoided

4.
AN OVERVIEW OF PROCEDURE

The remainder of this guide is concerned with the steps to follow to conduct an arbitration without legal representation. Clearly, you could be in a stronger position and feel more confident if you employed a Solicitor to present your case, but be aware that if you win, you will not be entitled to recover your legal costs. The small claims procedure is designed for self-representation.

The steps you must take to begin a County Court action against another person(s) are as follows:

Issue a Default Summons (fixed amount or damages to be assessed).

Two copies of the Summons must be taken to the Court Office and the Court Fee paid (see appendix 1). The court will then serve (i.e. post) the Summons on the Defendant with three forms, a Form of Admission (N9A), a form for filing a Defence (N9B) and a form for filing a Counterclaim (N9B). The Court will also:

- post to you a form called a "Plaint Note" (N205A). This form records the details of the claim, the case number and date of service. The case number is now the reference point for your case and no steps can be taken without quoting it

- you will also receive a Request for Judgement which is attached to the Plaint Note.

Two types of Summons are available, as follows:

- a Summons claiming a fixed sum of money, known as a "liquidated demand" - Form N1, or

- a Summons claiming damages to be assessed, where the court must assess and determine the level of compensation payable - Form N2

Court Service. The court will post the Summons to the Defendant with a Form of Admission, Defence and Counterclaim.

Forms of Admission
Defence and Counterclaim (Forms N9A and N9B)

The Defendant must return the Form of Admission (N9A), Defence and Counterclaim (N9B) to the Court within 14 days of the date of service printed on the summons. The Defendant has the following options:

Admission or Partial Admission

The Defendant may admit the whole claim by posting the Form of Admission direct to you. A request may be made for time to pay. You must then either accept or reject the request returning the Form of Admission to the court office with the Request for Judgement. The court will enter judgement but if the method of payment is rejected, the Court will enter judgement and set a date for a hearing to consider the method of payment.

If the defendant admits part of the claim, and you do not accept the sum offered, the offer may be rejected and the defendant must file a defence in respect of the balance. The court will set a date for an arbitration hearing.

Defence

If the Defendant files a Defence, you will receive a copy from the Court and the case is transferred to the Defendant's local court which will set a date for the Arbitration Hearing. *If you expect the defendant to file a defence, you will save time if you issue your Summons in his local County Court.* If a Defence is not filed within 14 days of service, you may return the Request for Judgement, and Judgement-in-Default will be entered in your favour. You will then receive a copy of the Judgement which will be in the form of an order for immediate payment or payment by instalments. This may be set aside on certain grounds which are discussed further on in this book.

Counterclaim

The defendant's counterclaim is a claim made by the Defendant against you which may be less than your claim, so your claim is reduced, or it may be greater. A counterclaim is a separate action. Rather than the Defendant issuing his own Summons, the dispute is managed in one set of proceedings by the defendant issuing a counterclaim. The Plaintiff is entitled to file a defence to the counterclaim. However, the Plaintiff is treated as having denied the allegations made in a counterclaim if a defence is not filed. Judgement-in-default is therefore not applicable to a counterclaim.

Date of the Arbitration Hearing

If a defence is filed, the court will set a date for the arbitration and issue directions - you will be notified by use of Form N18A. The Court must:

- ♦ give not less than 14 days notice of the date of the hearing, and

♦ issue directions before any hearing or pre-hearing

Directions Issued by the Court

When you are notified of the date of the hearing, you will also receive directions, which is the court instructions how the case will proceed. District Judges have wide powers to issue directions and local courts have their own practise. The purpose of directions is to ensure that the trial runs smoothly. The directions for an arbitration printed on Form N18A are usually limited to two:

♦ not less than 14 days before the date fixed for the hearing, each party must post to the other copies of any documents they intend to rely on at the hearing, and

♦ not less that 7 days before the hearing, a copy of any expert report on which each party intends to rely must be posted to both the court and the other party

Disclosure of Evidence

Each side is required to disclose the documents and expert reports before the hearing. This means supplying copies of the documents you propose to produce to prove your case, such as expert reports or a written contract or signed delivery note, to the defendant before the hearing.

Enforcement Proceedings

If the Defendant does not comply with the Judgement, which is a Court Order, you will be entitled to take enforcement proceedings which are discussed further on in this book.

Now please read the **KEY POINTS** from chapter 4 overleaf.

KEY POINTS

♦ the plaintiff must take the initiative and issue a default Summons. The plaintiff pursues the claim throughout This includes obtaining judgement and, if the defendant does not observe the judgement, enforcement proceedings

♦ the defendant's role is mainly reactive — but if there is no reaction, the plaintiff may be entitled to a default judgement

♦ a default judgement can be set aside by the court

5.
THE PLAINTIFF

This chapter explains how to complete a Summons form. A copy of the two Summons forms for a default action are appended to this chapter.

Plaintiff's Name & Address. The Summons form requires your full address (box 1), or if a company, the address of the registered office.

Defendant's Address. The defendants full name & address or if a Company the address of the Registered Office (box 3). This is found on the company's headed notepaper or by telephoning Companies House in Cardiff on 0222-388588. If the business is a partnership state (A Firm) after the name or a sole trader, state the full name and "Trading as (trade name)." Box two is only completed when a solicitor is acting on your behalf.

Category of Claim. A brief description of what your claim is for is required in the next box. This means stating what the claim consists of, for example, breach of contract, dishonoured cheque, non-payment of an invoice, or bad workmanship.

Particulars of Claim. In the case of a Default Action, the claim must be for a payment of money which could be either:

- A fixed monetary sum (known as a "liquidated Demand"), for example a debt, non-payment of a cheque (dishonoured cheque) or for breach of contract where the amount of damages for the Defendant's failing to comply with the contract is stated in the contract — known as a liquidated sum. Another example of a fixed amount is where you have purchased a product (eg washing machine) which does not work or is not fit for its purpose and you reject the product and claim back the purchase price. In this case, use form N1 printed at the end of this chapter.

♦ An amount which is not fixed but needs to be assessed (known as an "unliquidated demand"), for example, the washing machine could have leaked and damaged the carpet or you could have suffered a minor personal injury such as a broken finger which heals. In such a case, the amount of compensation needs to be assessed because the value of the carpet is a question of opinion rather than an obvious fact. In this case, use form N2 printed at the end of this chapter.

Particulars

The Particulars of your claim must be set out in the largest box or on a separate piece of paper. It is important to use numbered paragraphs and to set out each point relevant to your case.

For example, if you had a contract with the Defendant, and delivered goods, you must state or "plead" that:

♦ there was a written/oral contract between the plaintiff and defendant giving the date of the contract

♦ the relevant terms of the contract, for example, for the supply and delivery of goods/services

♦ that you performed your side of the contract, i.e. you delivered the goods/services

♦ the goods were accepted by the Defendant

- you issued an invoice for payment within 30 days

- the Defendant in breach of contract has not paid

AND LASTLY, you must state what you claim:

- payment of the invoice (state the amount), and

- interest at the contractual rate or statutory rate (currently 8%)

The main principles are outlined, but each Summons will be different depending on the claim. It will be easier to use numbered paragraphs for each statement or particulars of your claim.

What to do Next

Take the two copies of the completed summons form to the court and pay the issue fee. Remember to keep a copy for yourself. The court may ask for copies. The court will stamp the summons form and post it to the defendant with forms of admission, defence and counterclaim, explained in the next chapter. The defendant must reply to your summons within 14 days from the date of service printed on the Plaint Note. A company has 16 days to reply.

If the Defendant files a defence, the court will post a copy to you. A form of Admission is returned direct to the Plaintiff.

Obtaining Judgement in Default

Meanwhile, you will receive a Plaint Note from the Court with a Request for Judgement-in-Default attached (Form N18A). A copy is annexed to this chapter. If a defence is not filed, (you will know because the court will inform you if one is received,) complete and return the Request for Judgement to the court.

Accepting an Admission and Offer of Payment

As explained in the next chapter, the court serves a summons on the defendant with a form of Admission Defence and Counterclaim. If the defendant admits the claim, the form of admission is posted direct to you, the plaintiff. You must then complete and return it to the court requesting judgement and an order for payment. You may request judgement but object to the method of payment, or accept a part admission but pursue the balance in respect of which the defendant should file a defence and/or counterclaim.

If the Defendant admits the claim but asks for time to pay, you may reject the proposal. In the event of a dispute, the court staff will set an amount with reference to the information supplied by the defendant. The order to pay is issued on form N30(2), but if you object to the level of instalments, you are entitled to make an application to the district judge using form N244 for him to set a level of instalments. The case is then transferred to the defendant's local court for a hearing.

Now please read the **KEY POINTS** from chapter 5 overleaf.

KEY POINTS

When a Defence is filed, the case is transferred from the court where the summons was issued to the defendant's local court. If you expect the Defendant to file a Defence, you should consider issuing the Summons by posting it to the Defendants local court to avoid the time delay in the court transferring the case to that Court. Otherwise, a Default Summons may be issued in any County Court.

Forms Appended

    I.   Default summons - fixed amount (Form N1)

    II. Default summons - unspecified amount (Form N2)

    III. Notice of Issue of a Default Summons and Request for Judgement (Form N205A)

    IV. Notice of Arbitration Hearing and Judge's Directions (Form N205A)

A Straightforward Guide to Small Claims in the County Court

County Court Summons

Case Number *Always quote this*

In the

                                                    County Court

The court office is open from 10am to 4pm Monday to Friday

(1)
Plaintiff's
full name
address

(2)
Address for
service (and)
payment
(if not as above)
Ref/Tel no.

Telephone:

Seal

(3)
Defendant's
name
address

This summons is only valid if sealed by the court
If it is not sealed it should be sent to the court.

What the plaintiff claims from you

Brief
description
of type of
claim

Particulars of the plaintiff's claim against you

                          Amount claimed

                        Court fee

                        Solicitor's costs

                        Total amount

                        Summons issued on

What to do about this summons

You can

- dispute the claim
- make a claim against the plaintiff
- admit the claim in full and offer to pay
- pay the total amount shown above
- admit only part of the claim

**For information on what to do or if you
need further advice, please turn over.**

Signed
Plaintiff('s solicitor)
(or see enclosed particulars of claim)

N1 Default summons (fixed amount) (Order 3, rule 3(2)(b))

Keep this summons, you may need to refer to it

The Plaintiff

You have 21 days from the date of the postmark to reply to this summons
(A limited company served at its registered office has 16 days to reply.)

If you do nothing	Judgment may be entered against you without further notice.
If you dispute the claim	Complete the white defence form (N9B) and return it to the court office. The notes on the form explain what you should do.
If you want to make a claim against the plaintiff (counterclaim)	Complete boxes 5 and 6 on the white defence form (N9B) and return the form to the court office. The notes at box 5 explain what you should do.
If you admit all of the claim and you are asking for time to pay	Fill in the blue admission form (N9A). The notes on the form explain what you should do and where you should send the completed form.
If you admit all of the claim and you wish to pay now	Take or send the money to the person named at box (2) on the front of the summons. If there is no address in box (2), send the money to the address in box (1). Read How to Pay below.
If you admit only part of the claim	Fill in the white defence form (N9B) saying how much you admit, then **either:** Pay the amount admitted as explained in the box above; **or** Fill in the blue admission form (N9A) if you need time to pay

Interest on Judgments

If judgment is entered against you and is for more than £5000, the plaintiff may be entitled to interest on the total amount.

Registration of Judgments

If the summons results in a judgment against you, your name and address may be entered in the Register of County Court Judgments. **This may make it difficult for you to get credit.** A leaflet giving further information can be obtained from the court.

Further Advice

You can get help to complete the reply forms and information about court procedures at any county court office or citizens' advice bureau. The address and telephone number of your local court is listed under "Courts" in the phone book. When corresponding with the court, please address forms or letters to the Chief Clerk. Always quote the whole of the case number which appears at the top right corner on the front of this form; the court is unable to trace your case without it.

How to pay	To be completed on the court copy only
• PAYMENT(S) MUST BE MADE to the person named at the address for payment quoting their reference and the court case number.	Served on
• DO NOT bring or send payments to the court. THEY WILL NOT BE ACCEPTED.	By posting on
• You should allow **at least 4** days for your payments to reach the plaintiff or his representative.	
• Make sure that you keep records and can account for all payments made. Proof may be required if there is any disagreement. It is not safe to send cash unless you use registered post.	Officer
• A leaflet giving further advice about payment can be obtained from the court.	Marked "gone away" on
• If you need more information you should contact the plaintiff or his representative.	

A Straightforward Guide to Small Claims in the County Court

County Court Summons

| Case Number | *Always quote this* |

In the _____ **County Court**

The court office is open from 10am to 4pm Monday to Friday

Telephone

Plaintiff's full name address

Plaintiff's Solicitor's address

Ref/Tel No.

seal

Defendant's full name (including title e.g. Mr, Mrs or Miss) and address

This summons is only valid if sealed by the court. If it is not sealed it should be sent to the court.

Keep this summons, you may need to refer to it.

What the plaintiff claims from you

Give brief description of type of claim

Particulars of the plaintiff's claim against you

Amount claimed	see particulars
Court fee	
Solicitor's costs	
Total Amount	

Summons issued on _____

What you should do

You have 21 days (16 days if you are a limited company served at your registered office) from the date of the postmark to either

- **defend the claim** by filling in the back of the enclosed form and **sending it to the court;**

  OR

- **admit the claim** and make an offer of payment, by filling in the front of the enclosed reply form and **sending it to the court.**

If you do nothing judgment may be entered against you.

My claim is worth   £5000 or less ☐   over £5000 ☐

All cases over £1000

I would like my case decided by   trial ☐   arbitration ☐

Please read the information on the back of the form. It will tell you more about what to do.

Signed
Plaintiff or plaintiff's solicitor
(or see enclosed "Particulars of claim")

N2 Default summons (amount not fixed) (Order 3, rule 3(2)(b))

The Plaintiff

Please read this page : it will help you deal with the summons

If you dispute all or part of the claim
You may be entitled to help with your legal costs. Ask about the legal aid scheme at any county court office, citizens' advice bureau, legal advice centre or firm of solicitors displaying the legal aid sign.
- Say how much you dispute in the part of the enclosed form for defending the claim and return it to the court. The court will tell you what to do next.
- If you dispute only part of the claim, you should also fill in the part of the form for admitting the claim and pay the amount admitted into court.
- If the court named on the summons is not your local county court, and/or the court for the area where the reason for the claim arose, you may write to the court named asking for the case to be transferred to the county court of your choice. You must explain your reasons for wanting the transfer. However, if the case is transferred and you later lose the case, you may have to pay more in costs.

How the claim will be dealt with if defended
If the claim is worth £1,000 or less it will be dealt with by arbitration (small claims procedure) unless the court decides the case is too difficult to be dealt with in this informal way. Costs and the grounds for setting aside an arbitration award are strictly limited. If the claim is for £1,000 or less and is not dealt with by arbitration, costs, including the costs of help from a legal representative, may be allowed.
If the claim is worth over £1000 it can still be dealt with by arbitration if either you or the plaintiff asks for it and the court approves. If your claim is dealt with by arbitration in these circumstances, costs may be allowed.

If you want to make a claim against the plaintiff
This is known as a counterclaim
Fill in the part of the enclosed form headed 'Counterclaim'. If your claim is for more than the plaintiff's claim you may have to pay a fee - the court will let you know. Unless the plaintiff admits your counterclaim there will be a hearing. The court will tell you what to do next.

If you admit the claim or any part of it
- **You may pay an appropriate amount into court** to compensate the plaintiff (see Payments into Court box on this page), accompanied by a notice (or letter) that the payment is in satisfaction of the claim. If the plaintiff accepts the amount paid he is also entitled to apply for his costs.
- **If you need time to pay,** complete the enclosed form of admission and give details of how you propose to pay the plaintiff. If your offer is accepted, the court will send an order telling you how to pay. If it is not accepted, the court will fix a rate of payment based on the details given in your form of admission and the plaintiff's comments. Judgment will be entered and you will be sent an order telling you how and when to pay.
- **If the plaintiff does not accept the amount paid or offered,** the court will fix a hearing to decide how much you must pay to compensate the plaintiff. The court will tell you when the hearing, which you should attend, will take place.

General information
- If you received this summons through the post the date of service will be 7 days (for a limited company at its registered office, the second working day) after the date of posting as shown by the postmark.
- You can get help to complete the enclosed form and information about court procedures at any county court office or citizens' advice bureau. The address and telephone number of your local court is listed under 'Courts' in the phone book.
- Please address forms or letters to the Chief Clerk.
- Always quote the whole of the case number which appears at the top right corner of the front of this form; the court is unable to trace your case without it.

Registration of judgments
If the summons results in a judgment against you, your name and address may be entered in the Register of County Court Judgments. **This may make it difficult for you to get credit.** A leaflet giving further information can be obtained from the court.

Interest on judgments
If judgment is entered against you and is for more than £5000, the plaintiff may be entitled to interest on the total amount.

Payments into Court

You can pay the court by calling at the court office which is open 10 am to 4 pm Monday to Friday
You may only pay by:
- cash
- banker's or giro draft
- cheque supported by a cheque card
- cheque (unsupported cheques may be accepted, subject to clearance, if the Chief Clerk agrees)

Cheques and drafts must be made payable to HM Paymaster General and crossed.
Please bring this form with you.

By post
You may only pay by:
- postal order
- banker's or giro draft
- cheque (cheques may be accepted, subject to clearance, if the Chief Clerk agrees).

The payment must be made out to HM Paymaster General and crossed.
This method of payment is at your own risk.
And you must:
- pay the postage
- enclose this form
- enclose a self addressed envelope so that the court can return this form with a receipt

*The court **cannot** accept stamps or payments by bank and giro credit transfers.*

Note: You should carefully check any future forms from the court to see if payments should be made directly to the plaintiff

---

To be completed on the court copy only
Served on:
By posting on:
Officer:
This summons was returned by the Post Office marked 'Gone Away' on:

N2 Default summons (amount not fixed)

A Straightforward Guide to Small Claims in the County Court

Notice of Issue of Default Summons - fixed amount

To the plaintiff ('s solicitor)

Your summons was issued today. The defendant has 14 days from the date of service to reply to the summons. If the date of postal service is not shown on this form you will be sent a separate notice of service (Form N222).

The defendant may either
- Pay you your total claim.
- **Dispute the whole claim.** The court will send you a copy of the defence and tell you what to do next.
- **Admit that all the money is owed.** The defendant will send you form of admission N9A. You may then ask the court to send the defendant an order to pay you the money owed by completing the request for judgment below and returning it to the court.
- **Admit that only part of your claim is owed.** The court will send you a copy of the reply and tell you what to do next.
- **Not reply at all.** You should wait 14 days from the date of service. You may then ask the court to send the defendant an order to pay you the money owed by completing the request for judgment below and returning it to the court.

In the	WOOLWICH County Court
The court office at	THE COURT HOUSE, POWIS STREET, LONDON SE18 6JW, is open between 10 am & 4 pm Monday to Friday Tel: 081-854 2127
Case Number *(Always quote this)*	
Plaintiff *(including ref.)*	
Defendants	
Issue date	
Date of postal service	
Issue fee	£

For further information please turn over

Request for Judgment

- Tick and complete either A or B. Make sure that all the case details are given and that the judgment details at C are completed. Remember to sign and date the form. Your signature certifies that the information you have given is correct.
- If the defendant has given an address on the form of admission to which correspondence should be sent, which is different from the address shown on the summons, you will need to tell the court.

A ☐ The defendant has not replied to my summons
Complete all the judgment details at C. Decide how and when you want the defendant to pay. You can ask for the judgment to be paid by instalments or in one payment.

B ☐ The defendant admits that all the money is owed
Tick only **one** box below and return the completed slip to the court.

☐ **I accept the defendant's proposal for payment**
Complete all the judgment details at C. Say how the defendant intends to pay. The court will send the defendant an order to pay. You will also be sent a copy.

☐ **The defendant has not made any proposal for payment**
Complete all the judgment details at C. Say how you want the defendant to pay. You can ask for the judgment to be paid by instalments or in one payment. The court will send the defendant an order to pay. You will also be sent a copy.

☐ **I do NOT accept the defendant's proposal for payment**
Complete all the judgment details at C and say how you want the defendant to pay. Give your reasons for objecting to the defendant's offer of payment in the section overleaf. Return this slip to the court **together with the defendant's admission N9A** (or a copy). The court will fix a rate of payment and send the defendant an order to pay. You will also be sent a copy.

I certify that the information given is correct

Signed .... Dated ....

In the	WOOLWICH County Court
Case Number *(Always quote this)*	
Plaintiff	
Defendant	
Plaintiff's Ref.	

C Judgment details
I would like the judgment to be paid
☐ (forthwith) *only tick this box if you intend to enforce the order right away*
☐ (by instalments of £ .... per month)
☐ (in full by ....)

Amount of claim as stated in summons (including interest at date of issue) ....
Interest since date of summons (if any) ....
Period .... Rate .... %

Court fees shown on summons ....
Solicitor's costs (if any) on issuing summons .....
Sub Total
Solicitor's costs (if any) on entering judgment
Sub Total
Deduct amount (if any) paid since issue ....
Amount payable by defendant

N205A Notice of issue (default summons) and request for judgment (Order 3, rule (2)(d)(1), Order 9 rules 3 and 6) MCR 600279/K94142 11/91

Page 32

The Plaintiff

Further information

- The summons must be served within 4 months of the date of issue (or 6 months if leave to serve out of the jurisdiction is granted under Order 8, rule 2). In exceptional circumstances you may apply for this time to be extended provided that you do so before the summons expires.

- If the defendant does not reply to the summons or if he delivers an admission without an offer of payment you may ask for judgment. If you do not ask for judgment within 12 months of the date of service the action will be struck out. It cannot be reinstated.

- You may be entitled to interest if judgment is entered against the defendant and your claim is for more than £5000.

- You should keep a record of any payments you receive from the defendant. If there is a hearing or you wish to take steps to enforce the judgment, you will need to satisfy the court about the balance outstanding. You should give the defendant a receipt and payment in cash should always be acknowledged. You should tell the defendant how much he owes if he asks.

- **You must inform the court IMMEDIATELY if you receive any payment before a hearing date or after you have sent a request for enforcement to the court.**

Objections to the defendant's proposal for payment

Case Number

A Straightforward Guide to Small Claims in the County Court

Notice of Arbitration Hearing

Plaintiff

Defendant

In the	**Woolwich** County Court
Case No. *Always quote this*	
Plaintiff's Ref.	
Date	6 March 1995

To the plaintiff and defendant

1. Details of Hearing

This case is to be dealt with by arbitration under the small claims procedure. The notes overleaf tell you more about the hearing and what you need to do before it takes place.

The arbitration hearing will take place at **The Court House, 165-167 Powis Street, Woolwich, SE18 6JW**.

on , at

The time allowed for the arbitration is hours, minutes

If you do not attend, the district judge (the arbitrator) may make decisions in your absence.

If you do not wish your case to be dealt with under the informal small claims procedure, you may apply to the court. You should use form N244 which you can get free from the court office. You must say why you object to your case being dealt with as a small claims case.

The court will give you an appointment at which the district judge will consider your objections. If your case is not dealt with under the small claims procedure, costs may be allowed. That means, if you lose the case you may have to pay the other party's costs which may include the costs of help from a legal representative.

2. District Judge's Directions (What you should do)

(i) **Not less than 14 days before the hearing,** you must send the other party a copy of all the documents you have which you are going to use to prove your case.

(ii) **Not less than 7 days before the hearing,** you must send the court and the other party:
(a) a copy of any expert report you are going to use to prove your case and
(b) the name(s) and address(es) of any witness(es) you intend to use.

The court office at Woolwich County Court, The Court House, 165-167 Powis Street Woolwich SE18 6JW is open between 10 am and 4 pm Monday to Friday. When corresponding with the court, please address forms or letters to the Chief Clerk and quote the case number. Tel: 081 854 2127

Notice of arbitration hearing (small claims procedure) (Order 19, Rule 3)   N18A

3. Help and Advice

- You may find it helpful to get advice about your claim and the evidence you should produce at the hearing. Many solicitors will give up to half an hour's advice for a fixed fee of £5, or you may be entitled to advice under the Legal Advice and Assistance Scheme. If expert evidence would help to prove your claim, your local Citizens Advice Bureau may be able to suggest the name of a suitable person to provide a report. They may also offer more general advice and assistance.

- You may take someone with you to the hearing to speak for you. They cannot come to the hearing alone. This person is called a 'lay representative' and can be anyone you choose, for example, your husband or wife, a relative, friend, or advice worker.

- Some lay representatives may want to be paid for helping you. You should make sure you know exactly how much this will be. Consider carefully whether your claim is worth paying that amount. Remember, you will have to pay this yourself.

- You should also remember that some lay representatives who charge for their services may not belong to any professional body. This means that if you are dissatisfied with the way they handle your case, there may be no one to whom you can complain.

- Small claims leaflet number 6 ('A defence to my claim - what happens now?') and leaflet number 7 (An arbitration hearing - how do I prepare?) will give you more information about the hearing and what you have to do.

4. Notes on the arbitration hearing

- Arbitration is an informal way of dealing with a claim. The hearing is normally held in private.

- At the hearing the district judge (the arbitrator) will decide on the best way to:
  - identify the facts and matters in dispute, and
  - make sure you have a fair and equal opportunity to present your case.

- The strict rules of evidence will not apply. The arbitrator may take into account any evidence as long as it is fair to both parties to do so.

- If you do not attend the hearing, the arbitrator will normally deal with the case in your absence. But any documents you have sent to the court will be taken into account.

- If you have a lay representative, remember to give the arbitrator form Ex83 at the beginning of the hearing. (The arbitrator can tell your lay representative to leave if he thinks he or she is behaving badly).

- If you do not have anyone to speak on your behalf, you can ask the arbitrator to help by putting questions for you.

- At the end of the hearing, the arbitrator will tell you the decision and the reasons for it.

- The decision ('award') made at the hearing is normally final. You can apply to have it set aside, but the grounds (reasons) for doing so are **very limited.**

6.
THE DEFENDANT

This chapter examines the position of a defendant. As explained above, a Default Summons is served by the Court with a form of Admission Defence and Counterclaim. These forms are appended to this chapter.

If you receive a default summons claiming less than £1,000, the Plaintiff will be claiming a liquidated sum (form N1) or an unliquidated sum (Form N2). If you do not reply by returning the Form of Admission Defence & Counterclaim, the Plaintiff will be entitled to file the Request for a Default Judgement attached to the Plaint Note. The Court will enter "judgement-in-default" against you - meaning that the Court will order you to either:

- ♦ pay the liquidated sum demanded, or
- ♦ in the case of an unliquidated sum, judgement will be entered against you but with damages to be assessed, with reference to the evidence given by the Plaintiff at the hearing

The effect of filing a Defence to a Default Summons is that a hearing will be ordered and the Plaintiff loses the right to a default judgement.

Forms of Admission, Defence & Counterclaim

These three forms are served on you with a Summons. Examples are appended to this chapter. You have three options, as follows.

Form of Admission

If you admit the claim for the sum demanded, you may complete the form of Admission and post it to the Plaintiff:

- ♦ with payment, or
- ♦ with an offer for payment by instalments

The effect of an admission is that the plaintiff will be entitled to judgement in respect of the amount you admit. The issue then is the method of payment and whether the plaintiff or the court will sanction payment by instalments. You may admit part only of the claim if you believe that the plaintiff is not entitled to the whole amount but in such a case, you must use the forms of defence and/or counterclaim to resist the balance of the claim. If an admission is filed but the Plaintiff does not accept your offer to pay by instalments, the court staff will set an amount with reference to the information supplied by the defendant. The order to pay is issued on form N30(2), but if you object to the level of instalments, you are entitled to make an application to the district judge using form N244 for him to set a level of instalments. The case is then transferred to your local court for a hearing.

Form of Defence

If you admit only part of the claim, and the plaintiff does not accept your offer of part payment or rejects your offer of instalments, or deny that the claim is valid, you must file a Defence.

Preparing the Defence

The principle to follow in writing the defence is "admit what you admit and deny what you deny". Use numbered paragraphs to deal with each allegation in the Particulars written in the Summons. A denial means that the Plaintiff must prove an allegation; for example, that there was a contract, or that monies were not paid. An admission means that the Plaintiff does not have to prove a particular point.

It is important to make your own allegations against the Plaintiff (if any) in the Counterclaim and not the defence. The Counterclaim must demand some form of relief, e.g. damages.

Form of Counterclaim

If you wish to make a claim against the Plaintiff, you may file a Counterclaim. This is equivalent to issuing your own summons against the Plaintiff but is done by way of a Counterclaim rather than by issuing another Summons. The Counterclaim must be made in the same way as the Particulars contained in the Summons, with numbered paragraphs which state clearly what you claim and, finally, the compensation you require. You can claim a fixed amount, or damages to be assessed. If the Counterclaim is in excess of the "small claim" limit, the Court may dispense with the arbitration procedure and order a full hearing. A Court fee will be payable if the counterclaim exceeds the claim against you. The counterclaim is the equivalent of issuing a summons against the Plaintiff. Thus, while the defence answers the plaintiff's claim, the counterclaim is a separate action. The Plaintiff is entitled and should file a Defence & Reply to a counterclaim. However, the allegations in a counterclaim are treated as denied even if a Defence and Reply is not filed.

Setting Aside a Default Judgement

If a Default Judgement is made against you when you have a defence, you may apply to the Court for the judgement to be "set aside" by using form N244, but you must establish grounds for the application, for example, that you have a defence or that you did not receive the summons in the post. The court will arrange an arbitration hearing. You must give reasons for your failure to file a defence and convince the judge that your defence is genuine.

Third Party Proceedings

A defendant who holds a third party responsible for the Plaintiff's loss is entitled to join the third party in the action by issuing a Third Party Notice. Leave of the court is required to issue the Notice if the defence has been filed.

Now please read the **KEY POINTS** from chapter 6 overleaf.

KEY POINTS

- if you receive a Summons, you must take the appropriate action or judgement will be issued against you

- if judgement is entered, you can apply for it to be set aside. This means that you have permission to enter a defence

- if you think that you have a claim against the Plaintiff, you must complete the form of counter claim to make your claim. Do not make the claim in your Form of Defence

- if you admit the claim but believe that another person is responsible, you can issue Third Party Proceedings. This involves a degree of legal technicality and legal advice should be obtained

Forms Appended

I. Form of Admission Defence & Counter Claim (Form N9A)

II. Form of Defence & Counter Claim (Form N9B)

A Straightforward Guide to Small Claims in the County Court

Admission

When to fill in this form
- Only fill in this form if you are admitting all or some of the claim **and** you are asking for time to pay
- If you are disputing the claim or you wish to pay the amount claimed, read the back of the summons

How to fill in this form
- Tick the correct boxes and give as much information as you can. **Then sign and date the form.**
- Make your offer of payment in box 11 on the back of this form. **If you make no offer the plaintiff will decide how you should pay.**
- You can get help to complete this form at **any** county court office or citizens' advice bureau.

Where to send this form
- **If you admit the claim in full**
  Send the completed form to the address shown at box (2) on the front of the summons. If there is no address in box (2) send the form to the address in box (1).
- **If you admit only part of the claim**
  Send the form **to the court** at the address given on the summons, together with the white defence form (N9B).

What happens next
- **If you admit the claim in full and offer to pay**
  If the plaintiff accepts your offer, judgement will be entered and you will be sent an order telling you how and when to pay. If the plaintiff does **not** accept your offer, the court will fix a rate of payment based on the details you have given in this form and the plaintiff's comments. Judgement will be entered and you will be sent an order telling you how and when to pay.
- **If you admit only part of the claim**
  The court will tell you what to do next.

How much of the claim do you admit?
- [ ] I admit the full amount claimed as shown on the summons **or**
- [ ] I admit the amount of $ _____

1 Personal details
Surname: _____
Forename: _____
- [ ] Mr [ ] Mrs [ ] Miss [ ] Ms
- [ ] Married [ ] Single [ ] Other (specify)
Age: _____
Address: _____
Postcode: _____

In the WOOLWICH County Court
Case Number (Always quote this): _____
Plaintiff (including ref.): _____
Defendant: _____

2 Dependants (people you look after financially)
Number of children in each age group
under 11 [ ] 11-15 [ ] 16-17 [ ] 18 & over [ ]
Other dependants (give details): _____

3 Employment
- [ ] I am employed as a _____
  My employer is _____
  Jobs other than main job (give details) _____
- [ ] I am self employed as a _____
  Annual turnover is .... $
  - [ ] I am not in arrears with my national insurance contributions, income tax and VAT
  - [ ] I am in arrears and I owe .... $
  Give details of:
  (a) contracts and other work in hand
  (b) any sums due for work done
- [ ] I have been unemployed for ____ years ____ months
- [ ] I am a pensioner

4 Bank account and savings
- [ ] I have a bank account
  - [ ] The account is in credit by ...... $
  - [ ] The account is overdrawn by.... $
- [ ] I have a savings or building society account
  The amount in the account is .... $

5 Property
I live in
- [ ] my own property
- [ ] jointly owned property
- [ ] rented property
- [ ] lodgings
- [ ] council property

N9A Form of admission and statement of means to accompany Form N1 (Order 9, rule 2)   MCR 601757 5/94 C

The Defendant

6 Income

My usual take home pay *(including overtime, commission, bonuses etc)*	$	per
Income support	$	per
Child benefit(s)	$	per
Other state benefit(s)	$	per
My pension(s)	$	per
Others living in my home give me	$	per
Other income *(give details below)*		
	$	per
	$	per
	$	per
Total income	$	per

7 Expenses

(Do not include any payments made by other members of the household out of their own income)

I have regular expenses as follows:

Mortgage *(including second mortgage)*	$	per
Rent	$	per
Community charge	$	per
Gas	$	per
Electricity	$	per
Water charges	$	per
TV rental and licence	$	per
HP repayments	$	per
Mail order	$	per
Housekeeping, food, school meals	$	per
Travelling expenses	$	per
Children's clothing	$	per
Maintenance payments	$	per
Others *(not court orders or credit debts listed in boxes 9 and 10)*		
	$	per
	$	per
	$	per
Total expenses	$	per

8 Priority debts

(This section is for arrears only. Do not include regular expenses listed in box 7.)

Rent arrears	$	per
Mortgage arrears	$	per
Community charge arrears	$	per
Water charges arrears	$	per
Fuel debts: Gas	$	per
Electricity	$	per
Other	$	per
Maintenance arrears	$	per
Others *(give details below)*		
	$	per
	$	per
Total priority debts	$	per

9 Court orders

Court	Case No.	$	per

Total court order instalments	$	per

Of the payments above, I am behind with payments to *(please list)*

10 Credit debts

Loans and credit card debts *(please list)*

	$	per
	$	per
	$	per

Of the payments above, I am behind with payments to *(please list)*

11 Do you wish to make an offer of payment?

- *If you take away the totals of boxes 7, 8 and 9 and the payments you are making in box 10 from the total in box 6 you will get some idea of the sort of sum you should offer. The offer you make should be one you can afford.*

☐ I can pay the amount admitted on ____
or
☐ I can pay by monthly instalments of $ ____

12 Declaration

I declare that the details I have given above are true to the best of my knowledge

Signed ____   Dated ____

Position *(firm or company)* ____

A Straightforward Guide to Small Claims in the County Court

Defence and Counterclaim

In the WOOLWICH **County Court**

Case Number _Always quote this_

Plaintiff _(including ref.)_

Defendant

The court office is open from 10am to 4pm Monday to Friday

COURT HOUSE
165 POWIS STREET
WOOLWICH
LONDON
SE18 6JW

When to fill in this form
- Only fill in this form if you wish to dispute all or part of the claim **and/or** make a claim against the plaintiff (counterclaim).

How to fill in this form
- Please check that the correct case details are shown on this form. You must ensure that all the boxes at the top right of this form are completed. You can obtain the correct names and numbers from the summons. The court cannot trace your case without this information.
- Follow the instructions given in each section. Tick the correct boxes and give the other details asked for.
- If you wish only to make a claim against the plaintiff (counterclaim) go to section 5.
- Complete and sign section 6 before returning this form.

Where to send this form
- Send or take this form immediately to the court office at the address shown above.
- If you admit part of the claim and you are asking for time to pay, you will also need to fill in the blue admission form (N9A) and send **both** reply forms to the court.
- Keep the summons and a copy of this defence; you may need them.

Legal Aid
- You may be entitled to legal aid. Ask about the legal aid scheme at any county court office, citizen's advice bureau, legal advice centre or firm of solicitors displaying this legal aid sign.

What happens next
- If you complete box 3 on this form, the court will ask the plaintiff to confirm that he has received payment. If he tells the court that you have not paid, the court will tell you what you should do.
- If you complete box 4 or 5, the court will tell you what you should do.
- If the summons is not from your local county court, it will automatically be transferred to your local court.

1 How much of the claim do you dispute?

☐ I dispute the full amount claimed _(go to section 2)_

or

☐ I admit the amount of £ _____ and I dispute the balance

If you dispute only part of the claim you must **either**:
- pay the amount admitted to the person named at the address for payment in box (2) on the front of the summons or if there is no address in box (2), send the money to the address in box (1) (see How to Pay on the back of the summons). Then send this defence to the court.

or

- complete the blue admission form and send it to the court with this defence.

Tick whichever applies

☐ I paid the amount admitted on _____

or

☐ I enclose the completed form of admission

(go to section 2)

2 Arbitration under the small claims procedure
How the claim will be dealt with if defended

If the claim is for **£1,000 or less** it will be dealt with by arbitration (small claims procedure) unless the court decides the case is too difficult to be dealt with in this informal way. Costs and the grounds for setting aside an arbitration award are strictly limited. If the claim is for £1,000 or less and is not dealt with by arbitration, costs, including the costs of a legal representative, may be allowed.

If the claim is for **over £1,000** it can still be dealt with by arbitration if either you or the plaintiff asks for it and the court approves. If the claim is dealt with by arbitration in these circumstances, costs may be allowed.

Please tick this box if the claim is worth over £1,000 and you would like it dealt with by arbitration. ☐

(go on to section 3)

3 Do you dispute this claim because you have already paid it? _Tick whichever applies_

☐ No _(go to section 4)_

☐ Yes I paid £ _____ to the plaintiff on _____ _(before the summons was issued)_

Give details of where and how you paid it in the box below _(then go to section 6)_

N9B Form of defence and counterclaim to accompany Form N1 (Order 9, rule 2)   MCR 601757 5/94 C

Page 44

The Defendant

Case No.

4 If you dispute the claim for reasons other than payment, what are your reasons?
Use the box below to give full details. *(If you need to continue on a separate sheet, put the case number in the top right hand corner.)*

5 If you wish to make a claim against the plaintiff (counterclaim)

If your claim is for a specific sum of money, how much are you claiming? £

- If your claim against the plaintiff is for more than the plaintiff's claim against you, you may have to pay a fee. Ask at your local court office whether a fee is payable.

- You may not be able to make a counterclaim where the plaintiff is the Crown (e.g. a Government Department). Ask at your local county court office for further information.

What are your reasons for making the counterclaim?

- Use the box opposite to give full details.
(If you need to continue on a separate sheet, put the case number in the top right hand corner.)

(go on to section 6)

6 Signed
(To be signed by you or by your solicitor)

Position
(firm or company)

Dated

Give an address to which notices about this case can be sent to you

Postcode

7.
ISSUES OF EVIDENCE

Our legal system is in general adversarial and not inquisitorial. This means that both parties to a dispute must present a case to a judge and the judge decides in favour of one or the other. A judge, although an experienced lawyer, acts as an impartial observer. *The arbitration procedure is the exception to this rule.* The plaintiff must still prove a case, but in an arbitration, the judge will be more involved and will ask questions. The "spade work" is the responsibility of the plaintiff who prepares a case to be presented to the judge. In an arbitration, the judge acts as an arbiter, which means that he takes a role in assisting the parties to find a compromise. If no compromise is possible, the judge will decide whether the Plaintiff has proved the case against the Defendant. In the case of a counterclaim, the defendant must prove a case against the plaintiff.

Types of Evidence

There are essentially two types of evidence:

- Oral evidence, and
- Material evidence

Oral evidence is the matter(s) you and your witnesses (if any) can report to the judge because these matters are known by you personally, and is first hand evidence. Material evidence is the evidence which is not oral, such as documentary evidence like a contract or delivery note, or an object. For example, you could take an electrical item which is not working to court in order to prove that it does not work. The object itself is evidence.

How to Use Your Evidence

In proving your case, two "rules" of evidence are important. First, the Plaintiff must prove a case - this is called the "burden of proof" — and as each side makes allegations, the allegations must be answered — this is called the "onus of proof". The Plaintiff has the burden of proving the case against the defendant "on the balance of probabilities". This means that the judge must be satisfied that your case is more likely to be "right" than the defendant's case. However, the defendant is required to answer the allegations made or the judge will accept that the claim is proven.

Burden of Proof

Neither party to a dispute can provide 100% proof. The Plaintiff must prove the case "on the balance of probabilities", which means that the judge must be convinced that, with reference to the evidence you produce, the facts which you allege or what you say has happened is "more likely than not". You must also prove the level of your financial loss so that the Court can assess the compensation (known as "damages") you should receive. If the Defendant files a defence, you as the Plaintiff must prove your case to the satisfaction of the Judge.

Onus of Proof

As you present your arguments, the "onus of proof" moves from one side to the other. For example, you may produce evidence that goods were delivered but not paid for. The other side will try and prove that goods were paid for. The onus of proof moves from one side to the other. The defendant may then produce evidence of payment. The onus of proof returns to the Plaintiff. The Plaintiff could allege that the payments were for other invoices and so on. In assessing whether you have proved your case, the judge will pay careful attention to these arguments and whether one case is stronger that the other. If the arguments are of equal strength, the judge must dismiss the Summons. If your case is stronger than the defence, the judge will make orders against the defendant in your favour. In effect, you must "discharge the burden of proof".

What You Must Prove

At the hearing, the plaintiff must prove each of the statements made in your Particulars of Claim, and the level of loss you have suffered. The defendant must prove his allegations in the counterclaim. The purpose of damages is to compensate the Plaintiff for loss, not to punish the defendant. In a contractual dispute, this means placing the Plaintiff as far as possible in the financial position he would have been in had the defendant correctly performed the contract.

The Particulars the plaintiff does not have to prove are those admitted by the defendant in the defence. For example, in the case of the Particulars for breach of contract listed in chapter 5 the defence could:

- ♦ admit that there was a contract
- ♦ admit that the goods were delivered

But in his defence:

- ♦ claim that the goods were not accepted, and/or
- ♦ allege that they were of inferior or unmerchantable quality or unfit for their purpose, as is required by the Sale of Goods Act, 1979

In all cases, the Plaintiff must prove that the defendant received the Summons. This is relevant when the defendant does not attend the hearing or attends but denies service, but is not relevant when the defendant has returned one of the forms of admission, defence and counterclaim.

In the above example, the Plaintiff must prove that the goods were accepted. The defendant would have to produce evidence to prove that the goods were of merchantable quality, but you will give evidence to contradict this evidence or produce evidence of your own, for example, a signed delivery note, correspondence, or evidence to show that the defendant did not raise the issue of quality before you issued the Summons or made pressing demands for payment.

Proof of Loss

You being the Plaintiff (or the Defendant in respect of a Counterclaim), must prove by giving evidence that the matters alleged have caused financial loss. The object of damages is to put the plaintiff in the position he would have been in had a breach of contract not occurred, or in the case of physical injury, to put the plaintiff in the financial position he would have been had the injury not occurred. Compensation therefore would cover loss of earnings as well as for physical discomfort.

Types of Evidence

The facts behind your arguments may be proved by a combination of oral and documentary evidence. Oral evidence will be given by yourself and the Defendant, and any witnesses who support your case.

Documentary Evidence

To prove your case, you may be relying on documentary evidence, such as a signed contract, a Delivery Note, a returned cheque, or correspondence. Photocopies of the documents which you intend to use to prove your case must be served on the defendant at an agreed time before the hearing. Remember to comply with the courts directions (see chapter 4).

Witness Evidence

Witnesses may be asked to give evidence of the facts you need to prove. You will be giving oral evidence at the trial and you may wish to call others to give evidence of fact. If a witness is unwilling to attend the hearing, you are entitled to compel attendance by issuing a witness summons (Form N20).

Expert Evidence

An arbitration is intended to be informal and not overburdened by procedure. However, you (or the defendant) may require expert evidence to prove your case. Expert evidence is required where an opinion must be given - rather that evidence of fact. An "expert" must be acceptable to the Court. Expert evidence is usually given only after the expertise has been established, eg by stating academic qualifications. Producing expert evidence requires the expense of an expert's report, for example, proving that a product purchased was unfit for some reason. The defendant may also call an expert to give evidence in support of the defence or to challenge your expert evidence. Expert evidence must also be exchanged before the hearing, as explained in chapter 4 above. The expert should be called to give oral evidence at the arbitration hearing and to explain and elaborate on his report.

Costs of Witness and Experts

The reasonable expenses of a party travelling to a hearing are allowed, up to a maximum of £29. The costs of an expert report up to a maximum of £112.50 are recoverable by the successful party.

Now please read the **KEY POINTS** from chapter 7 overleaf.

KEY POINTS

- at the hearing, the Plaintiff must present a case. The judge is not there to do this for you. His role is to arbitrate and decide who has the strongest case

- "small claims" arbitrations do not follow the strict rules of evidence and court procedure, although the basic undercurrent of these rules apply. This is because complicated legal issues rarely have a role to play in a claim below £1,000. The main issues are usually the facts and, in general, a determined plaintiff can work out what facts are relevant and how to prove them. Due to the informal nature of "small claims" and to encourage legal representation to be dispensed with, the judge will be prepared to adopt a less passive role in a "small claims" arbitration

- the ease with which you can prove a case depends to a great extent on the documentary evidence you have. It is therefore important to have an administrative system which guarantees clear correspondence, signed contracts, and signed delivery notes

- the judge will decide on the basis of the oral evidence and documents presented to him, and the law

- legal costs are not awarded but certain costs may be awarded in favour of the successful party

8.
PREPARING FOR THE ARBITRATION HEARING

Before an arbitration, both sides must disclose the evidence that they propose to present to the judge prior to the hearing. Certain formal steps are necessary before the hearing. The Court controls the pre-hearing steps by issuing "directions". The usual directions for an arbitration are listed in chapter 4.

Pre-Trial Reviews and Directions

If directions listed in chapter 4 are not adequate, either party may make an application for the court to hold a "pre-trial review" at which a party may request additional directions. The district judge also has wide powers to make directions or, if the presence of the parties is required, to order a pre-arbitration hearing. Such a hearing is likely if the judge feels that the summons does not establish a claim, or if the defence does not present a proper defence. In an Arbitration, for the less complicated cases, the directions listed in chapter 4 should be sufficient. However, either party may apply for directions using the form N244 at any stage in the case and a date will be scheduled at which you may give arguments for the directions you are seeking. The defendant may oppose your application or not attend the hearing. In nearly all cases, the Court will grant any directions which both parties request. It is usual where possible to agree directions by consent. Both parties write to the court asking for the same direction; for example, permission to amend the pleadings. Such steps are unlikely to be necessary for a "small claim".

A hearing for directions is informal and takes place in a private room with a district judge and the litigants present.

Failure to Attend a Pre-Arbitration Appointment

If the Plaintiff fails to attend, the judge would most likely strike the case out. If the defendant does not attend, the judge could either issue directions or strike out the defence, or if the admission is filed, allow the plaintiff to prove the level of loss suffered.

Exchange of Evidence

The court's directions require expert reports and documentary evidence to be exchanged. If either side fails to abide by these directions, the other side may apply for an order that he shall be prevented from relying on such evidence at the Arbitration hearing. You may have to make the application during the hearing as disclosure is required only seven or fourteen days beforehand.

Trial Date

If not done already, the Court will set a date for the trial. The judge who issues the directions gives a time estimate of how long he expects the case to last. If the time estimate is too short, or if you cannot attend on the appointed day, write to the court and/or telephone the listings clerk.

Consent Orders

The Court will normally approve a settlement which both sides accept. This is achieved by a Consent Order. A formal form of consent may be signed and filed with the Court any time before the hearing. In a small claim arbitration, it would be sufficient for both sides to write to the court outlining their agreement or for one party to set out the agreed compromise and the other to sign at the foot of the letter. A consent order must be approved by the judge.

At the hearing, if a compromise is agreed, the judge would record the agreement so that a consent order or judgement is drawn up by the court.

Withdrawing the Summons

If a settlement has been agreed, the Plaintiff may file a Notice of Discontinuance (Form N297) and a certificate saying that the defendant has been informed of withdrawal of the Summons. The case would be ended without a court order. This option may be suitable if the Plaintiff simply abandons the case altogether, or if the defendant pays an agreed sum in one payment. If instalments are agreed, the Plaintiff is better off with a court order which is capable of enforcement. A consent order would be preferable to a discontinuance.

Now please read the **KEY POINTS** from chapter 8 overleaf.

KEY POINTS

- be careful to comply with any directions

- failure to exchange documentary evidence and expert reports may mean that you cannot use such evidence during the arbitration hearing

- if you cannot attend on the appointed day or if the time estimate is too short, write to the chief clerk and telephone the listing clerk

- the safest way to settle a case is by a consent order. The order will help with enforcement

- the case could also be settled by filing a Notice of Discontinuance (Form N279)

9.
Arbitration & Judgement

You will receive notification of the date for the Arbitration Hearing from the Court when the Defence is filed. Cases are listed in blocks, for example, a number of cases will be listed for 10.00 AM and will be heard in order. The hearing will usually be listed for half an hour.

When you arrive on the day, you will find a list of the day's cases on a notice board. Check that your case is listed (yourself-versus-the Defendant) and inform the usher that you have arrived. The usher will know if the defendant has arrived and will know if he or she is represented by a solicitor.

If you consider it worthwhile, you could discuss the dispute with the Defendant before the hearing. If you achieve a compromise, the Judge would most likely approve it at the hearing and issue a consent order. Ensure that the Defendant has received all the documents you or the court have served on him.

The usher will show you into the judge's private room. The judge will usually be sitting at the end of a long table. You and the Defendant will sit on either side. The witnesses should be asked to wait outside to be called when required. The correct way to address a judge is "Sir" or "Madam".

As the Plaintiff, you must present your case at the hearing. This means you must speak in a semi-public forum, but only the parties and the judge will be present. It may help you to prepare notes of what you propose to say before the hearing. The actual conduct of the arbitration is at the discretion of the judge, but Rule 19(2) reproduced in Appendix 2 sets out the parameters.

The main points of your arguments must be foremost in your mind if you are to give a good impression.

How to Present Your Case - The Plaintiff

The judge will have a copy of the summons, defence and counterclaim. Ask the judge if he or she has all the court documents, the Summons, Particulars of Claim, and the Defence. Take the judge through the Particulars of Claim to explain your case. Identify the points admitted by the Defendant in the Defence.

Having given an outline of your case, introduce the evidence you have to support it. This would most likely be oral evidence from yourself, but you may have witnesses, although this is not essential and not usual for a "small claim". Each witness should be called from the waiting room individually to be questioned by yourself and the Defendant. In an Arbitration, it is likely that the judge will question them himself. The process is meant to be informal. You may produce an expert report and call the expert as a witness to give oral evidence. Expert witness are usually called to give oral evidence, unless the defendant has accepted the evidence in the report.

The judge will try to mediate and thus find an agreed solution. The extent to which the judge takes an active role varies between judges.

How to Present Your Case - The Defendant

You will speak after the Plaintiff's opening remarks. Address the points made by the Plaintiff with reference to the Particulars of Claim. Present your Defence, as outlined in the defence you filed. If you have filed a Counterclaim, this must be presented as though you were a plaintiff. You are aslo entitled to call witnesses and present expert evidence.

The judgement on a counterclaim will be served with judgement on the summons as explained above.

Failure to Attend

If the Plaintiff fails to attend, the judge could decide that there is no case to answer and dismiss the summons. In such a case, the plaintiff could apply for judgement to be set aside if grounds exist. If the Defendant fails to attend, the judge could enter judgement for the Plaintiff or decide that there is no case to answer and dismiss the summons.

Judgement

If a compromise is not possible, the judge will decide on the evidence whether the Plaintiff has proved the case and is entitled to the orders requested. The judge will usually make a decision on the claim and counterclaim (if any) at the hearing. Be careful to write down what the judgement is. The court will prepare the form of judgement and serve it on both sides. If it is inaccurate or incorrect, contact the court immediately.

Setting Aside a Default Judgement

If judgement is made against you when you are not present, an application can be made within 14 days for judgement to be set aside and the case proceed to another arbitration. Form N244 should be used and reasons must be given.

Now please read the **KEY POINTS** from chapter 9 overleaf.

A Straightforward Guide to Small Claims in the County Court

KEY POINTS

- at the hearing you must present your case, because the plaintiff has the burden of proof. The judge will be concerned to decide whether the facts you rely on, such as delivery of goods, have been proven, eg by producing a signed delivery note

- the defendant must answer your case, because the onus of proof will require him or her to give some explanation. A counter-claim must be argued in the same way as a claim

10.
ENFORCEMENT PROCEDURES

It is often assumed that after the court judgement is issued, no further action is required. This is so if the damages are paid or the Defendant abides by any court orders. However, a Judgement Debtor does not always co-operate. You must then take enforcement proceedings if the debtor does not comply with a court order. If ordered to pay by instalments, failure to pay an instalment means that the outstanding balance becomes due.

Orders for the payment of monetary compensation may be enforced in a number of ways.

Enforcement Proceedings – Money Judgements

To enforce a judgement, an appropriate method of enforcement must be chosen and enforcement procedure followed. *The orders below are available to a judgement creditor but please read the free leaflet supplied by the court before taking any action.*

Oral Examination (Form N37/38)

The court orders the defendant to attend a hearing and answer your questions on oath concerning his income and assets. Your objective is to find something to use to satisfy the debt with use of the orders mentioned below.

Attachment of Earnings (Form N337)

The Court orders the defendant's employer to deduct monies from salary and pay such monies into court. The court will then pay you. This enforcement method is used to enforce payment of instalments and is applicable to judgement debts of over £50. This order can only be made by the defendant's local court and you may need to apply for your case to be transferred. The application (Form 337) is served on the debtor with a form of reply and the debtor has eight days to reply. A court officer will then make an attachment of earnings order based on the information received.

Warrant of Execution (Form N323)

The Court authorises its bailiff to seize the defendant's property for sale. If the debtor wishes to make an arrangement with the creditor, the warrant may be suspended using form N245. If the creditor objects, a hearing before the district judge will be arranged.

Garnishee Order (Forms N349)

The Court orders a person who owes money to or holds money on behalf of the defendant, such as a bank or building society, to pay such monies into court. You are responsible for the administrative costs of the bank or building society in complying with the order. The order will be confirmed at a subsequent hearing.

Charging Order (N86/87)

The court orders a mortgage or charge to be registered over freehold or leasehold property or property such as securities and shares as security for payment. You must prove that the debtor owns the property. In the case of land, this means obtaining "Office Copy Entries" from H. M. Land Registry for which you would need to complete a "Public Index Map" search to find out the title number of the land.

Enforcement Procedures

Order for Sale

The Court orders the sale of property subject to a charging order.

The following methods of Enforcement Exist but you should obtain advice before attempting them yourself.

Appointment of a Receiver

The court may on your application appoint a receiver to collect a sum due at a future date such as rent, royalties, payment under an insurance policy or savings plan.

Bankruptcy Proceedings

The non-payment of damages in breach of a court order constitute grounds for you to issue a bankruptcy petition against the judgement debtor.

Choice of Method of Enforcement

The most suitable method for enforcing a judgement is apparent from the defendant's answers to an Oral Examination, the Defendant's circumstances, or the type of asset you aim to enforce judgement against.

An Attachment of Earnings is aimed at a judgement debtor who is employed and who has been ordered to pay by instalments. The warrant of execution against goods and garnishee orders are to enforce immediate orders to pay. A charging order is for property which can not be "removed" by a bailiff, such as land stocks and shares, where the important factor is the name on the company's share register. A court may make a charging order on the home of a judgement debtor but orders for sale are rare. However, where the debt is substantial and the property is the only asset of the judgement debtor, the court may authorise a charging order and order sale. The charge over land, like a mortgage, must be registered at H.M. Land Registry, for which the services of a solicitor are essential.

Procedure for Obtaining Enforcement Orders

Each method of enforcement is supported by a standard application form. An *oral examination* requires a hearing. An application for an *attachment of earnings* order will result in a hearing, prior to which the debtor receives the date of the hearing and a form to complete.

An application for a *garnishee order* must be sworn as an oath, the form itself is an affidavit. This may be sworn before the court official. The court will then make an interim order called a "garnishee order nisi" and set a date for a hearing to consider whether the garnishee order will be made absolute. The debtor and/or third party will have an opportunity to argue that the order should not be made absolute. Meanwhile, within eight days of the garnishee order nisi, the bank may pay the monies held on account of the debtor into court and you will have an opportunity to accept or reject the payment in. If the payment is less than the judgement debt, you are not prevented from pursuing the balance.

An application for an *attachment of earnings order* can only be made by the defendant's local court and you may need to apply for your case to be transferred. The application (Form N337) is served on the debtor with a form of reply and the debtor has eight days to reply. A court officer will then make an attachment of earnings order based on the information received. Before issuing enforcement proceedings, discuss the steps required with the court personnel and read the the free booklet "Enforcing Money Judgements" supplied by the court.

Now please read the **KEY POINTS** from chapter 10 overleaf.

KEY POINTS

- winning judgement may not be the end of the case but instead lead you into yet further court proceedings

- debtors prisons have been abolished - but there are a number of options for enforcing a judgement

- choose an appropriate method of enforcement and remember that you must convince a judge that the order should be made

- remember that a debtor with no assets is a "man of straw" and is not going to pay up no matter what you do.

Forms Appended

I. Application for an Oral Examination (Form N316)

II. Application for an Attachment of Earnings Order (Form N337)

III. Application for a Garnishee Order (Form N349)

Request for Oral Examination

to be completed and signed by the plaintiff or his solicitor and sent to the court with the appropriate fee

1 Plaintiff's name and address

In the

County Court

Case Number

2 Name and address for service and payment
(if different from above)
Ref/Tel No.

For court use only

O/E no.

Issue date:

3 Defendant's name and address

Hearing date:

on

at   o'clock

at (address)

4 Name and address of person to be orally examined if different from Box 3

(ie director of defendant company)

5 Judgment details

Court where judgment/order made if not court of issue

I apply for an order that the above defendant (the officer of the defendant company named in Box 4) attend and be orally examined as to his (the defendant company's) financial circumstances and produce at the examination any relevant books or documents

6 Outstanding debt

you may be able to claim interest if judgment entered for more than £5000 on or after 1 July 1991

Balance of debt and any interest*/damages at date of this request

Issue fee

AMOUNT NOW DUE

Unsatisfied warrant costs

I certify that the balance now due is as shown

Signed

Plaintiff (Plaintiff's solicitor)

Dated

IMPORTANT
You must inform the court immediately of any payments you receive after you have sent this request to the court

N316 Request for oral examination (Order 25, rule 3(1A)   Dd 8365073 300M 1/92 Ed(297150)

Request for Attachment of Earnings Order
To be completed and signed by the plaintiff or his solicitor and sent to the court with the appropriate fee

1 Plaintiff's name and address

In the

County Court

Case Number

2 Name and address for service and payment *(if different from above)* Ref/Tel No.

for court use only

A/E application no.

Issue date:

Hearing date:

on

at   o'clock

at (address)

3 Defendant's name and address

4 Judgment details

Date of judgment/order

Court where judgment/order made if not court of issue

I apply for an attachment of earnings order

I certify that the whole or part of any instalments due under the judgment or order have not been paid and the balance now due is as shown

5 Outstanding debt

Balance due at date of this request

Issue fee

AMOUNT NOW DUE

Signed

Plaintiff (Plaintiff's solicitor)

Unsatisfied warrant costs

Dated

6 Employment Details *(please give as much information as you can)*

Employer's name and address

Please proceed with this application in my absence
(delete if for maintenance or otherwise appropriate)

Defendant's place of work *(if different from employer's address)*

IMPORTANT
You must inform the court immediately of any payments you receive after you have sent this request to the court

The defendant is employed as

Works No/Pay Ref.

IN THE	COUNTY COURT
	CASE No.

BETWEEN .... PLAINTIFF

AND .... DEFENDANT

AND .... GARNISHEE

(1) Insert full name address and occupation of deponent.

I,⁽¹⁾

[Solicitor for] the above-named plaintiff, make Oath and say:—

1. That I [or on the   day of   19   , obtained a judgment [or an order] in this court against the above-named defendant for payment of the sum of £   for debt [or damages] and costs.

2. That £   is still due and unpaid under the judgment [or order].

3. That to the best of my knowledge or belief the garnishee,

of

(2) Add where appropriate.

is indebted to the defendant [in the sum of £   ]⁽²⁾ [for payment of which sum the defendant obtained a judgment [or order] in the   County Court against the garnishee on the   day of   19   , and by the judgment [or order] it was ordered that the garnishee should pay the sum of £   into the office of the court on the   day of   19   , [or by instalments of £   for every   ], and the sum of £   remains due and unpaid under the judgment [or order].]⁽²⁾

4. That the garnishee is a deposit taking institution having more than one place of business [and the name and address of the branch at which the defendant's account is believed to be held is

and the number of the account is believed to be   ] OR [I do not know at which branch the defendant's account is held, or what the number of the account is.]⁽²⁾

5. That the last known address of the defendant is

Sworn at   in the
of   this
day of   19

Before me _____

Officer of a Court, appointed by the Judge to take Affidavits.

This affidavit is filed on behalf of the plaintiff.

N.349   Affidavit in support of application for garnishee order

GLOSSARY OF IMPORTANT TERMS

Action	The name given to legal proceedings
Attachment of Earnings	Enforcement of a judgement debt by deducting payments from salary or earnings
Bailiff	The court officer who enforces warrents of execution. Also used to serve documents
Burden of Proof	The term which means that the plaintiff must prove his case. A case made by way of counterclaim
Charging Order	Enforcement of a judgement by a mortgage over property belonging to the debtor
Chief Clerk	The head administrator of the court to whom all letters should be addressed
Case reference	The number given to each case which must be quoted on all
Counterclaim	A separate claim made by the defendant against the plaintiff

County Court	The civil court which conducts arbitrations of small claims
Damages	The legal term for the compensation the court orders the successful party to pay the unsuccessful party
Default summons	A type of summons or action which allows the plaintiff judgement without a hearing if the defendant does not file a defence
Defendant	The party who is sued
Defence	The rejection of a claim filed by the defendant
Directions	Court orders informing the parties of any preliminary action to take before the arbitration
District Judge	The judge who will act as arbiter at the arbitration of the small claim
Evidence	The process by which the facts of a case are established, for the benefit of the judge. Evidence may be oral or documentary

Glossary of Important Terms

Expert	A person who has an expertise which is recognised by the court
Expert evidence	Evidence given by an expert to support a case, consisting of an expert report and oral evidence
Form of Admission	The court form used by the defendant to admit or partially admit a claim, and to offer payment by instalments
Form of Defence	The form used by the defendant to counterclaim file a defence or counterclaim
Garnishee Order	An enforcement order requiring a creditor of the judgement debtor to pay monies into court on account of the debt to the successful party
Judgement	The court's determination of a case ordering the parties to take certain action, usually a payment of money
Litigant	The plaintiff or defendant
Liquidated Sum	A fixed claim as opposed to an unknown claim

Onus of Proof	The obligation to answer or rebut allegations made by the other side
Open letter	A letter offering a settlement which is intended to be binding, compared to a "without prejudice" letter or offer
Oral Examination	An examination of a debtor on oath in court whereby the successful party asks questions with a view to choosing a suitable method of enforcement
Order for Sale	An order enforcing a charging order and is rare
Plaintiff	The party who starts an action
Plaint Note	The form received by the Plaintiff when a summons is issued
Pre-Trial Review	A pre-hearing ordered by the district judge, unusual in small claims
Prove	To give evidence which "on the balance of probabilities" shows that an argument is correct

Glossary of Important Terms

Request for Judgement	The form filed by the plaintiff when the summons is ignored
Service	Delivering court documents to the other side
Small Claim	A monetary claim of less than £1,000
Unliquidated Sum	A claim for damages to be assessed, where the exact amount is not known
Warrant of Execution	Enforcement whereby the court bailiff seizes goods belonging to the debtor for sale
Without prejudice	An offer which is not binding

APPENDIX 1

COURT FEES

Summons: To £599 – 10% of amount claimed minimum fee £10

£600 to £999 – £65

£1,000 to 5,000 – £70

Above £5,000 – £80

Oral examination: £30

Garnishee Order: £25

Charging Order: £25

Attachment of Earnings: 10% amount claimed
minimum £10
maximum £80

APPENDIX 2

ORDER 19

REFERENCE TO ARBITRATION
OR FOR INQUIRY AND REPORT
OR TO EUROPEAN COURT

1 **Interpretation and Application**

In this Part of this Order, unless the context otherwise requires -

lay representative means a person exercising a right of audience by virtue of an order made under section 11 of the Courts and Legal Services Act 1990 (representation in county courts),

reference means the reference of proceedings to arbitration under section 64 of the Act,

order means an order referring proceedings to arbitration under that section and

outside arbitrator means an arbitrator other than the judge or district judge.

2 **In this Part of this Order**

(a) Rules 3 and 4 apply only to small claims automatically referred to arbitration under rule 3, and

(b) Rules 5 to 10 apply to all arbitrations.

3 **Automatic Reference of Small Claims**

(1) Any proceedings in which the sum claimed or amount involved does not exceed £1,000 (leaving out of account the sum claimed or amount involved in any counterclaim) shall stand referred for arbitration by the district judge upon the receipt by the court of a defence to the claim.

(2) Where any proceedings are referred for arbitration by the district judge under paragraph (1), he may, after considering the defence and whether on the application of any party of his own

motion, order trial in court if he is satisfied -

>   (a) that a difficult question of law or a question of fact of exceptional complexity is involved; or
>
>   (b) that fraud is alleged against a party; or
>
>   (c) that the parties are agreed that the dispute should be tried in court; or
>
>   (d) that it would be unreasonable for the claim to proceed to arbitration having regard to its subject matter, the size of any counterclaim, the circumstances of the parties or the interests of any other person likely to be affected by the award.

(3) Where the district judge is minded to order trial in court of his own motion -

>   (a) the proper officer shall notify the parties in writing specifying on which of the grounds mentioned in paragraph (2) the district judge is minded to order trial in court;
>
>   (b) within 14 days after service of the proper officer's notice on him, a party may give written notice stating his reasons for objecting to the making of the order;
>
>   (c) if in any notice under sub-paragraph (b) a party so requests, the proper officer shall fix a day for a hearing at which the district judge -
>
>   >   (i) shall decide whether to order trial in court, and
>   >
>   >   (ii) may give directions regarding the steps to be taken before or at any subsequent hearing as if he were conducting a preliminary appointment or, as the case may be, a pre-trial review; and, in the absence of any request under sub-paragraph (c), the district judge may, in the absence of the parties, order trial in court.

(4) For the purposes of paragraph (1), 'a defence to the claim' includes a document admitting liability for the claim but disputing or not admitting the amount claimed.

4 Restriction on Allowance of Costs in Small Claims

(1) In this rule, 'costs' means -

(a) solicitors' charges;

(b) sums allowed to a litigant in person pursuant to Order 38, rule 17;

(c) a fee or reward charged by a lay representative for acting on behalf of a party in the proceedings.

(2) No costs shall be allowed as between party and party in respect of any proceedings referred to arbitration under rule 3, except -

(a) the costs which were stated on the summons or which would have been stated on the summons if the claim had been for a liquidated sum;

(b) the costs of enforcing the award, and

(c) such further costs as the district judge may direct where there has been unreasonable conduct on the part of the opposite party in relation to the proceedings or the claim therein.

(3) Nothing in paragraph (2) shall be taken as precluding the award of the following allowances -

(a) any expenses which have been reasonably incurred by a party or a witness in travelling to and from the hearing or in staying away from home;

(b) a sum not exceeding £29.00 in respect of a party's or a witness's loss of earnings when attending a hearing;

(c) a sum not exceeding £112.50 in respect of the fees of an expert.

(4) Where trial in court is ordered, paragraph (2) shall not apply to costs incurred after the date of the order.

(5) Where costs are directed under paragraph (2)(c), those costs shall not be, those costs shall not be taxed and the amount to be allowed shall be specified by the arbitrator or the district judge.

5 The Arbitrator

(1) Unless the court otherwise orders, the district judge shall be the arbitrator.

(2) An order shall not be made referring proceedings to the Circuit judge except by or with the leave of the judge.

(3) An order shall not be made referring proceedings to an outside arbitrator except with the consent of the parties.

(4) Where proceedings are referred to an outside arbitrator, the order shall be served on the arbitrator as well as on the parties, but it shall not, unless the court directs, be served on anyone until each party has paid into court such sum as the district judge may determine in respect of the arbitrator's remuneration.

6 Preparation for the Hearing

(1) Paragraph (2) of this rule shall apply unless the district judge -

    (a) is minded to order trial in court under rule 3 (3) or

    (b) decides that a preliminary appointment should be held.

(2) Upon the reference to arbitration the district judge shall consider the documents filed and give an estimate of the time allowed for the hearing and the proper officer shall -

    (a) give the parties not less than 21 days' notice of the day fixed for the hearing; and

    (b) issue directions under paragraph (3) in the appropriate form regarding the steps to be taken before or at any subsequent hearing.

(3) Where proceedings stand referred to arbitration, the following directions shall take effect -

    (a) each party shall not less than 14 days before the date fixed for the hearing send to every other party copies of all documents which are in his possession and on which that party intends to rely at the hearing;

(b) each party shall not less than 7 days before the date fixed for the hearing send to the court and to every other party a copy of any expert report on which that party intends to rely at the hearing and a list of the witnesses whom he intends to call at the hearing.

(4) A preliminary appointment shall only be held -

(a) where directions under paragraph (3) are not sufficient and special directions can only be given in the presence of the parties, or

(b) to enable the district judge to dispose of the case where the claim is ill-founded or there is no reasonable defence. In deciding whether to hold a preliminary appointment, the district judge shall have regard to the desirability of minimising the number of court attendances by the parties.

(5) Where the district judge decides to hold a preliminary appointment, the proper officer shall fix a date for the appointment and give to the plaintiff and the defendant not less than 8 days' notice of the day so fixed.

(6) On the preliminary appointment the district judge shall have the same powers as he has under Order 17 on a pre-trial review and he shall -

(a) give an estimate of the time to be allowed for the hearing (unless the parties consent to his deciding the dispute on the statements and documents submitted to him); and

(b) whether of his own motion or at the request of a party, give such additional directions regarding the steps to be taken before and at the hearing as may appear to him to be necessary or desirable. Dirrections given under sub-paragraph (b) may include (but shall not be limited to) a requirement that a party should clarify or, as the case may be, his defence.

(7) After the preliminary appointment, the proper officer shall -

(a) give the parties not less than 21 days' notice of the

day fixed for the hearing; and

(b) issue directions under paragraph (3) in the appropriate form regarding he steps to be taken before or at the hearing together with any additional directions given pursuant to paragraph (6)(b).

(8) The district judge may from time to time whether on application or of his own motion amend or add to any directions issued if he thinks it necessary to do so in the circumstances of the case.

(9) The following provisions of these rules shall not apply where proceedings stand referred to arbitration:

(a) Order 6, rule 7 (further particulars),

(b) Order 9, rule 11 (particulars of defence),

(c) Order 14, rules 1 (2), 3 to 5 5A and 11 (discovery and interrogatories), and

(d) Order 20, rules 2 and 3 (notices to admit facts and documents),

(e) Order 20, rule 12A (exchange of witness statements). Order 11, rules 1, 1A, 3 to 5, 7, 8 and 10 (payments into court) and Order 13, rule 1 (8) (a) (security for costs) shall not apply where proceedings stand referred to arbitration under rule 3.

(10) If it appears to the court at any time after a reference has been made (whether by order or otherwise) that there are any other matters within the jurisdiction of the court in dispute between the parties, the court may order them also to be referred to arbitration.

7 Conduct of Hearing

(1) Any proceedings referred to arbitration shall be dealt with in accordance with the following paragraphs of this rule unless the arbitrator otherwise orders.

(2) The hearing may be held at the court house, at the court office or at any other place convenient to the parties.

(3) The hearing shall be informal and the strict rules of evidence shall not apply; unless the arbitrator orders otherwise, the hearing shall be held in private and evidence shall not be taken on oath.

(4) At the hearing the arbitrator may adopt any method of procedure which he may consider to be fair and which gives to each party an equal opportunity to have his case presented; having considered the circumstances of the parties and whether (or to what extent) they are represented, the arbitrator -

> (a) may assist a party by putting questions to the witnesses and the other party; and

> (b) should explain any legal terms or expressions which are used.

(5) If any party does not appear at the arbitration, the arbitrator may, after taking into account any pleadings or other documents filed, make an award on hearing any other party to the proceedings who may be present.

(6) With the consent of the parties and at any time before giving his decision, the district judge may consult any expert or call for an expert report on any matter in dispute or invite an expert to attend the hearing as assessor.

(7) The arbitrator may require the production of any document or thing and may inspect any property or thing concerning which any question may arise.

(8) The arbitrator shall inform the parties of his award and give reasons for it to any party who may be present at the hearing.

8   Setting Awards Aside

(1) Where proceedings are referred to arbitration, the award of the arbitrator shall be final and may only be set aside pursuant to paragraph (2) or on the ground that there has been misconduct by the arbitrator or that the arbitrator made an error of law.

(2) Where an award has been given in the absence of a party, the arbitrator shall have power, on that party's application, to set the award aside and to order a fresh hearing as if the award were a judgement and the application were made pursuant to Order 37, rule 2.

(3) An application by a party to set aside an award by a district judge or an outside arbitrator on the ground mentioned in paragraph (1) shall be made on notice and the notice shall be served within 14 days after the day on which the award was entered as the judgement of the court.

(4) An application under paragraph (3) shall, giving sufficient particulars, set out the misconduct or error of law relied upon.

(5) Order 37, rule 1 (rehearing of proceedings tried without a jury) shall not apply to proceedings referred to arbitration.

9 Mode of Voluntary Reference

(1) Except as provided by rule 3, a reference shall be made only on the application a party to the proceedings sought to be referred.

(2) Unless the court otherwise directs, an application by a party to any proceedings or a reference may be made -

>(a) in the case of a plaintiff, by request incorporated in his particulars of claim;

>(b) in the case of a defendant, by request incorporated in any defence or counterclaim of his;

>(c) in any case, on notice under Order 13, rule.

(3) Where an application for a reference is made under paragraph (1) and the proceedings are not referred to arbitration under rule 3, the following provisions shall apply:

>(a) Subject to rule 5 (2) and sub-paragraphs (b) and (c) below, an order may be made by the district judge.

>(b) If the court is satisfied that an allegation of fraud against a party is in issue in the proceedings, an order shall not be made except with the consent of that party.

>(c) Where the district judge is minded to grant an application under paragraph (1), the proper officer shall notify the parties in writing accordingly and within 14 days after service of the proper officer's notice on him, a party may give written notice stating his reasons for objecting to the reference; if in any such notice a party so requests,

Order 19 - Reference to Arbitration

the proper officer shall fix a day for a hearing at which the district judge shall decide whether to grant the application and, in the absence of any such request, the district judge may consider the application in the absence of the parties.

10 Costs

Subject to rule 4, the costs of the action up to and including the entry of judgement shall be in the discretion of the arbitrator to be exercised in the same manner as the discretion of the court under the provisions of the County Court Rules.

APPENDIX 3

FORMS REPRODUCED IN THIS GUIDE

N1	Default Summons – fixed amount
N2	Default Summons – amount to be assessed
N205A	Notice of Issue of Default Summons & Request for Judgement
N18A	Notice of Arbitration Hearing & Judge's Directions
N9A	Form of Admission
N9B	Form of Defence & Counterclaim
N316	Application for an Oral Examination
N337	Application for an Attachment of Earnings Order
N349	Affidavit for a Garnishee Order